CROW
TALK

"As Counting Crows' number one fan, I arguably know everything about them. This did not stop me from being totally captivated by this in-depth, intimate, admirable look into the widely adored world of Counting Crows. A 'must have' for any fan."

— **Lisa (AnnaBegins.com)**

CROW TALK:

THE DEFINITIVE GUIDE TO COUNTING CROWS

Jessica Roop

ROCKET RIDE PRESS
PO Box 842, Hilliard, OH 43026
(614) 527-0458
www.rocketridepress.com

© 2001 by Jessica Roop

Printed in the United States of America

Published by:
Rocket Ride Press
PO Box 842
Hilliard, Ohio 43026 USA
Phone: (614) 527-0458
Fax: (775) 845-2029
Email: info@rocketridepress.com
Web: http://www.rocketridepress.com

Publisher's Cataloging–in–Publication Data
Provided by Quality Books, Inc.

Roop, Jessica.
    Crow talk : the definitive guide to Counting
Crows / Jessica Roop. – 1st ed.
    p. cm.
    Includes bibliographical references and
discography.
    LCCN: 00-190462
    ISBN: 0-9800162-0-4

    1. Counting Crows (Musical group) 2. Rock
groups. 3. Rock musicians.   I. Title.

ML421.C68R66 2000   782.42166'092'2
                    QBI00-500071

Dedication

This book is for the person who has made the most difference in my life: Brittany Stickel. Thank you for honestly being the best friend I have ever had. You've been there through the good, the bad, and the crazy. I know you'll always be there to wait next to Counting Crows' tour bus in a city in the middle of nowhere or to scream during "Ferris Wheel" at the latest Joe 90 show. You radiate.

And to all of the musicians whose music keeps me alive and inspired — Counting Crows, Joe 90, Live, Peter Stuart, Cracker, Gigolo Aunts, and so many more — I never will stop thanking you.

Contents

SECTION FOUR - Miscellaneous

SECTION FIVE - Photographs

Preface

I felt it was only fitting to try to explain why I have written this book. I cannot exactly explain how Counting Crows make me feel or even *why* they make me feel the way they do but I truly know it's the right way to feel. I have been a Counting Crows fan since July 11, 1997. Definitely not as long as many but long enough to feel the full scope of this band and their music. I know what it's like to have their music course through my veins and their lyrics echo in my head. I know the feeling of euphoria when they come out onstage and blast the songs throughout the venue effortlessly, painfully, and joyfully. I know the smile that spreads across my face when they perform on a television show or when one of their songs comes on the radio. They're certainly not *my* secret or *my* band but I still sometimes get that feeling inside of me that every person who hasn't stumbled upon Counting Crows is just going to keep stumbling. If everyone can't experience what I feel with Counting Crows, I sincerely hope they can experience it with someone or something. It's a feeling that can never quite be duplicated.

I must admit, I'm a whole band kind of girl. I care just as much about Ben Mize's drumming or Dan Vickrey's guitar playing as I do about Adam Duritz's singing. All of the band members are such an integral part of this big picture called Counting Crows. They fit together effortlessly, yet so much would be missing if they weren't all together. I could listen to Dave Bryson talk about guitars just as long as I could listen to Adam Duritz talk about lyrics. It's good to see them as a whole — when you stand back and watch them from afar, you can really see how important each and every band member is.

By writing this book, I'm not claiming to know everything about Counting Crows. I'm merely a seventeen-year-old fan who wants to tell the world just what's so special about these guys. No, a collection of facts can't convey all of the emotions that are conjured up every time I listen to their music, but maybe it can serve as a basis for showing why I am so interested in them. If you're not a Counting Crows fan yet, go buy yourself their albums and maybe, just maybe, you'll open up a door in your life. Or maybe you won't find a connection there. If not Counting Crows, maybe another band. Music is beautiful — don't let it slip through your fingers.

I wish I had a concrete explanation for this beautiful music. When I think about it, I realize that they are the one constant thing in my life. When you're a teenager, nothing seems constant. Friends aren't constant. Love isn't constant. Faith isn't constant. Trust isn't constant. Quite simply, life isn't constant. But I know there is one thing that is unfaltering — Counting Crows. Through everything in the past few years, their music has been there. They were there when I had spinal surgery; they were there when I was angry at the world; they were there when everything seemed perfect; they were there when everything seemed like a lie; they were there when I felt alone; and they were there when I felt euphoric. A line in "Mrs. Potter's Lullaby" talks about a piece of Maria existing in every song. I feel, like nearly every other Counting Crows fan, that there is a piece of *me* in every song.

So, please enjoy this book. Please contact me if you like it. Tell me why *you* fell in love with Counting Crows. Tell me about your first concert experience. Tell me about your favorite song. Maybe you can explain to me just what makes this band so incredibly special.

Jessica Roop

Section One

THE BAND

No matter how over-saturated the music world became
with "Mr Jones," it's still a classic. There's a certain
light you see in everyone's eyes when the opening notes
burst through the speakers.

Adam Duritz
vocals & piano

1 - The Basics

Full name: Adam Fredric Duritz

Born August 1, 1964.

Hometown: Baltimore, Maryland

He has also lived in El Paso, Texas; Boston, Massachusetts, Denver, Colorado; Houston, Texas; Oakland, California; and Berkeley, California.

He currently resides in Beverly Hills, California. He lived in the Hollywood Hills area prior to moving to Beverly Hills.

From the time he was a teenager until he moved to the Hollywood Hills in 1995, he lived in Berkeley, California.

His parents, Linda and Gilbert, are both doctors. His father is a neonatologist. His mother attended medical school in Mexico while Adam was a teenager. She is a geriatric psychiatrist.

His sister, Nicole, works at the American Association of Retired Persons.

He studied English at UC Berkeley, leaving just two credits shy of completing his degree. He didn't turn in his thesis on Hilda Doolittle.

Prior to studying at UC Berkeley, he attended UC Davis for two years.

Adam played soccer when he was younger and saw the Brazilian soccer team with his father.

II - The Road to Fame

The first song he wrote was "Good Morning Little Sister" when he was in college.

The first concert he attended was of Jackson Five.

When he was younger, he sang at Hebrew school and local bat mitzvahs.

A few of his earlier musical influences were Van Morrison, Bruce Springsteen, the Beatles, Big Star, R.E.M., and The Band. When he was a freshman in college, a literary influence was Carolyn Forché.

In addition to Counting Crows, he also sang in Mod-L Society, Himalayans, and Sordid Humor.

While he was trying to make it as a musician, he washed dishes, worked as a clerk in at a video store, worked in construction, and landscaped.

When trying to make it big in the late 1980s, Adam and David Immergluck lived in a warehouse on Fourth Street in Berkeley across from an ink factory. They'd watch *Twin Peaks* and think about becoming big stars.

Along with David Bryson, Adam formed Counting Crows in 1989. They played open-mic nights at bars and coffee-houses in the Bay Area.

III - Everything Else

During late 1994 and early 1995 when the band was taking time off before recording a new album, Adam worked as a bartender in Johnny Depp's Viper Room located in Los Angeles, California.

Adam took a portable DVD player on the road with him during the *This Desert Life* tour.

During the January 1993 performance at the Rock & Roll Hall of Fame ceremony, Adam didn't have his dreadlocks. A photograph of this can be seen in the June 1994 issue of Rolling Stone magazine.

Adam's dreadlocks are extensions. He likes them because they make him happy when he looks in the mirror. According to Charlie, his favorite hair joint is located in New Orleans.

He read a lot of comic books as a child.

Adam owned an indie record label called E Pluribus Unum that supported such bands as Duke Daniels, Gigolo Aunts, Joe 90, and Neilson Hubbard.

He enjoys reading books about the Civil War.

Adam tried acting for a while and was good at it; however, he didn't like taking orders.

During his early twenties, Adam had a problem with drugs. With the help of his family and friends, he was able to kick his addiction.

Adam has a hard time sleeping as highlighted in many of his song lyrics.

The band thinks Adam eats strange food — he has even eaten horsemeat.

Adam says the only things he knows how to do are sing and write music.

During a concert at the Beacon Theatre in New York, Adam jumped off a piano riser and tore his ACL in two and tore cartilage. He had to have reconstructive surgery. After injuring himself, he completed two more songs before he went off to get his knee wrapped. He also finished the concert.

Adam has soft nodes in his throat which occasionally flare up and cause show cancellations.

Adam co-executive produced a movie with Bryan Singer. The movie, "Burn," was shown at the Slamdance Film Festival.

Before "Burn," Adam and a few of his friends produced a movie called "The Locusts." Adam has never seen it.

Adam collects bootlegs of lots of different bands including the Beatles and Radiohead. He says he would be a hypocrite if he told people not to collect Counting Crows bootlegs since he owns so many bootlegs himself.

He's not a big fan of awards. He has stated that he feels it's all about the sales.

Adam posts on America Online's Counting Crows folder occasionally.

Adam dislikes the fact that "Einstein on the Beach" was released and so widely played. He says it was his experiment in pop music.

Adam refuses to play "Suffocate," an unreleased Counting Crows song. The only notable live performance of it was during a November 1995 Hollywood, California show.

His favorite band is said to be the Beastie Boys.

Adam refers to the stage as his house.

He often comes out on stage to sing with fellow tour mates. He has been known to sing on The Wallflowers' "Sixth Avenue Heartache," Gigolo Aunts' "The Big Lie," Joe 90's "Drive," Cracker's "Low," and Live's "The Dolphin's Cry."

It's easy to see the dedication in Counting Crows fans by just showing up at a general admission show. Fans line up for 7PM shows at 9AM just to guarantee themselves a front and center spot.

Dave Bryson
guitar

I - The Basics

Full name: David Lynn Bryson

Born October 5, 1961

Currently resides in Berkeley, California.

II - His Musical Talents

Dave's main guitar is a 1956 Les Paul Junior which can be seen in the "Angels of the Silences" video.

He also uses a Goldtop Les Paul, a 1960s Jetglo 360/12 Rickenbacker (as seen in the "A Long December" video), a 1961 Gretsch 6120, and a 1961 Jazzmaster.

For acoustics, he uses a mid-1950s Gibson J-45. He grew fond of vintage Gibson acoustics because of T-Bone Burnett, the producer of *August and Everything After*.

He prefers larger amps. He uses a Matchless DC-30 and Marshall Blues Breaker combo onstage.

He uses Ernie Ball strings on all of his electric guitars, except for his Rickenbacker 12-string, on which he uses Pyramid strings. He uses flatwounds on his Gretsch.

If he could only record with one mic, he would choose the Shure SM57.

For *Recovering the Satellites*, David picked up the National steel (a resophonic guitar).

David produced an album by Sordid Humor and mixed an album by Train.

III - Everything Else

Before Counting Crows, David was working as a recording engineer with producer Matt Wallace. He produced many albums himself including the demo for Adam's early band, Himalayans.

David met Adam in 1987 or 1988 and the two began playing together in 1989. This became the first incarnation of Counting Crows. The band broke up shortly after that and Adam began playing for Himalayans in 1990. David and Adam got back together for the second incarnation of Counting Crows in 1990 or 1991.

His favorite food is oysters.

Some of David's hobbies include windsurfing and golfing.

He writes the set lists for every show.

He owned Dancing Dog Studios, located in Emeryville, California.

One of David's friends, Tom Schindler, an acoustic engineer, helps the band optimize their rented houses for album recording.

Matt Malley and David first met in 1986 in a band called Mr. Dog.

He graduated from UC Berkeley with a degree in Humanities.

Someday when Counting Crows no longer exist, there will still be the memories to share. The late night rides into the darkness after a show, the utter joy of listening to an album for the first time, the haunting qualities of bootlegs from years past, and the friendships with everyone you have met along the way.

3

Charlie Gillingham
accordian & keyboard

I - The Basics

Full Name: Charles Thomas Gillingham

Born January 26, 1960 in Torrence, California but grew up in San Pedro, California.

Currently resides in San Francisco, California.

Married with one child.

Plays Hammond B-3, accordion, piano, Mellotron, Wurlitzer, guitar, and harmonica. He does all of the string arrangements.

II - The Road to Fame

He played trombone in his elementary school band.

He started out playing at high school dances, weddings and fraternity parties. His first show was a talent show in 1973.

Before joining the band, he had a promising career designing artificial intelligence in Silicon Valley.

Charlie met Adam in 1985 when Adam's first band opened for The Brambles, a band that Charlie later joined. Charlie was selling beer at the show.

III - His Musical Talents

He is probably most known for his red accordion, an instrument he bought for only $30 in Omaha, Nebraska. Fittingly, one of his key moments onstage with his red accordion is at the beginning of the song "Omaha."

He has made guest appearances on albums by Train, Cola, Cracker, Separate Ways, Peter Stuart, and American Music Club.

Charlie brought in a lot of the music for "Angels of the Silences" on *Recovering the Satellites*. He wrote almost all of "I Wish I Was a Girl."

He toured with Wire Train, opening for Bob Dylan in 1991.

In the mid-1980s, he played rockabilly and R&B in bands that toured Japan, Alaska, Canada, and the Pacific Northwest.

He has played one-off shows with Bo Didly, The Drifters, The Del Vikings, Mary Wells, and Chuck Berry.

He played in Patrick Winningham's band in San Francisco. Other members of the band were Dan Vickrey and Jeff Trott (Sheryl Crow's former guitar player). "Four White Stallions" and "Wiseblood" come from this band.

I - The Basics

Full Name: Matthew Mark Malley

Born July 4, 1963.

Currently resides in Thousand Oaks, California.

Married to Sesh with a son, Tansen.

II - The Road to Fame

One of his earlier jobs was washing windows. However, he wanted to be a fighter pilot or an air traffic controller.

He spent a year at Lambuth University in Tennessee.

He was the only male in an all-female bluegrass band.

In 1990, Matt was frustrated with his inability to succeed as a musician, so he sold all of his musical equipment, moved to Vancouver, and began painting houses.

He got involved with Counting Crows through David
Bryson, with whom he was in a band called Mr. Dog.

III - His Musical Talents

When he was growing up, he played along to Yes records on
a Rickenbacker 4001. In the late 1980s, he played
Steinbergers.

Currently, he mainly uses a 1961 stack-knob Fender Jazz
bass. He occasionally uses a 1960s Hoffner.

He has purchased a guitar from Santa Cruz Guitar Company.

He was nominated for a 1993 Bay Area Music Award in the
bassist category. Some of his contenders were Les
Claypool from Primus and Jack Blades from Damn
Yankees.

He helped write a lot of "A Murder of One."

IV - Everything Else

His favorite band is Led Zeppelin.

He has met John Paul Jones, the bassist for Led Zeppelin.

He likes to sing AC/DC's "Back in Black" during sound
check.

He was married in 1996 to his wife, whom he met in India.

Matt frequents America Online.

His favorite cereal is Count Chocula.

He likes to drink a special tea on the road that consists of raw ginger, basil leaves, black pepper, honey, and butter.

He had the song "El Scorcho" by Weezer on his answering machine for a long time.

He has been doing Sahaja Yoga since 1987.

"Greening of America" is his favorite song written by Adam.

Seeing Adam Duritz and Ed Kowalczyk from Live sing "The Dolphin's Cry" together was a moment like no other. Thirty seconds into the song, the lights went out; when they came back up, Adam barreled out from the back of the stage and the two sang the rest of song with such unbridled and intense passion.

1 - The Basics

Full Name: Benjamin G. Mize

Born February 2, 1971 in Durham, NC.

Currently resides in Georgia.

II - The Road to Fame

At the age of seven, Ben's first drum kit was a Christmas gift. Five hours after he brought it home, he broke it.

Five years later, he bought his second drum kit with money he earned through mowing lawns.

He purchased many drum magazines and books and played along with Van Halen to learn how to play.

He was a self-described work-a-holic when it came to teaching himself how to play the drums.

Some of his influences were John Bonham and Ringo Starr.

Ben and his family moved to Lilburn, Georgia in the mid-80s.

After high school, he moved to Athens, Georgia in 1989 where he sold coffee at Jittery Joe's Coffee Bar and worked as the monitor engineer at the Forty Watt Club. This is the same club where he met Adam.

In Athens, Georgia, he joined a surf band called The New Invincibles. His stage name was "Speedy."

He also played in the Athens, Georgia bands Redneck Grease Deluxe, Greenhouse, Daisy, Marlee MacLeod, and Clamp.

He was introduced to Counting Crows through Cracker, whom he toured with for six weeks during their *Kerosene Hat* tour.

Ben replaced former Counting Crows drummer Steve Bowman in 1994.

He was sent a copy of *August and Everything After* and a note to learn eighteen songs soon after his audition. He also listened to Counting Crows bootlegs to learn the rare songs.

His first show with Counting Crows was on September 23, 1994 at the Greek Theatre in Berkeley, California.

It's an instant connection. Each band member seems to know exactly what to do when and if another band member does this or that. The audience seems to be mesmerized by this band's amazing fluidity.

III - His Musical Talents

His drums are Gretsch and his cymbals are Zildjian. His hardware is Yamaha.

He played the Zippo lighter and light bulbs on *Recovering the Satellites*.

He played on Jars of Clay's 1999 album *If I Left the Zoo*.

IV - Everything Else

He said the best concert that he has attended was a R.E.M. show at the Forty Watt Club with only four hundred other people.

His favorite band is Cracker.

His former Rational Thinking professor, Steve J. Martin, from the University of Georgia in Athens, said that Ben was one of his best students.

Ben began college as a philosophy major. During his senior year, he changed his major to journalism.

Every Counting Crows fan has a story. Just ask them and they can tell you the exact place they were when they heard their first Counting Crows song on the radio or bought their first album. Every fan is so different yet they share one common bond: the music.

Dan Vickrey
guitar

I - The Basics

Full Name: Daniel John Vickrey

Born August 26, 1966 in Walnut Creek, California.

Currently resides in Los Angeles, California.

II - The Road to Fame

Dan began playing guitar in sixth grade with his first band that included Steve Bowman on drums.

He took his guitar lessons using a nylon-string guitar for a year before buying his first guitar, a Les Paul. He still owns this guitar and used it in the "Angels of the Silences" video.

His musical influences were The Beatles, John Mayall and the Blues Breakers featuring Eric Clapton, and B.B. King.

Before Counting Crows, he worked at several record stores including Tower and Village Music in Mill Valley.

He has a Political Science degree from University of California, Los Angeles.

In San Francisco, he played with a band called Naked Barbie Dolls which is now called Vagabond Dirt Lovers.

He was introduced to Counting Crows through Charlie Gillingham. The two had been in a band together with Patrick Winningham.

After releasing *August and Everything After* in 1993, Counting Crows decided that they wanted another guitar player for the tour. David Immergluck, who had played on the album, was slated to tour with the band but ended up deciding not to. Dan auditioned and made the band for the tour... and ended up staying for the long run.

Dan learned the songs in just one weekend.

III - His Musical Talents

Dan's main guitar is a 1954 Esquire. He owns four other Telecasters, including an original Fender Nocaster.

Some of his other favorite electric guitars include a 1956 Les Paul Junior, a 1956 Les Paul Special, and a Gretsch Duo-Jet. His Gretsch Duo-Jet was used on "Another Horsedreamer's Blues."

He used an old Gibson J-160E on *This Desert Life*. He was going to sell it because he thought that it sounded horrible, but he liked the way it sounded when he started playing it on that song.

He uses Ernie Ball strings on his guitars.

He originally wrote "Daylight Fading" while he was playing alone backstage in Glasgow, Scotland.

IV - Everything Else

The best concert he has attended was a Tom Waits show on New Years, 1989.

Dan saw Elvis Costello at dinner one night and tried to give him a flower which he had uprooted from the restaurant grounds. He was not given the warmest reception.

During the *August and Everything After* tour, Dan was often seen wearing peach air fresheners around his neck. He wore them until his mother told him that she thought they were "tacky." He now wears long-chained dog tags with rings given to him by various friends.

Some of his favorite artists are Tom Waits, The Beatles, Frank Sinatra, George Jones, and Bruce Springsteen.

During a December 1996 concert when Adam injured his knee, Dan sang "Wiseblood" while Adam's knee was being wrapped.

It's a wonderful feeling to drive for hours on end to a city you've never heard of and arrive at a venue you've never been to and to hear familiar songs quietly escaping from the cracks in the doors. You're swept with a great feeling of contentment to know that just beyond those locked doors lies a stage that will have your dreams poured upon it in a few hours.

I - Steve Bowman

Born January 14, 1967.

He is the former drummer for Counting Crows. He was released from the band in October 1994.

In the summer of 1991, Steve cut a demo with Adam, David Bryson, Charlie, and Matt.

After he left Counting Crows, he played with Third Eye Blind for a year before they became popular.

II - David Immergluck

He plays pedal steel, mandolin, electric guitar, and acoustic guitar.

He attended University of California, Santa Cruz for two years.

David met Adam when he did sound for one of Adam's bands in 1988 or 1989. Marty Jones reintroduced the two and they started Counting Crows together.

David has played on all three of Counting Crows' albums. He is pictured in the photo in the back of *August and Everything After* booklet, holding the cards.

He was originally supposed to tour with Counting Crows after the release of *August and Everything After* since he had contributed so much to the album and the band; however, he decided that it was not the thing that he wanted to be doing at that point in his life.

He toured with Counting Crows during their *This Desert Life* tour. Although never officially announced, David seems to now be a permanant fixture in the band's line-up.

He has played for Camper Van Beethoven, John Hiatt, Cracker, Sordid Humor, Dean Del Ray, The Ophelias, and Monks of Doom.

Section
Two

THE ALBUMS

There's a certain mystery that lies behind the lyrics to "August and Everything After" written on the album cover. It's the most elusive Counting Crows song and it seems as though everyone wants to see the rest of the lyrics and everyone wants to hear it. No one seems to know if that will ever come to be.

August & Everything After
Released 9-14-93

Produced by T-Bone Burnett

Songs: Round Here, Omaha, Mr. Jones, Perfect Blue Build-
ings, Anna Begins, Time and Time Again, Rain King,
Sullivan Street, Ghost Train, Raining in Baltimore, and A
Murder of One.

Singles: Mr. Jones, Round Here, and Rain King.

Music Videos: Mr. Jones and Round Here.

1 - The Charts

Album Chart debut: January 1, 1994

Album Chart Peak: Number 4 (April, 1994).

It stayed on the charts for 93 weeks.

Singles Chart Debuts: Mr. Jones - January 22, 1994; Round
Here - June 18, 1994; and Rain King - December 10,
1994.

Singles Weeks on Chart: Mr. Jones - 47; Round Here - 24; and Rain King - 4.

Over seven million copies have been sold in the United States; over ten million worldwide.

11 - The Songs

Adam had not yet visited Omaha when he wrote the song "Omaha." The band was later given a key to the city. The song was written in either 1984 or 1985 when Adam was twenty or twenty-one.

During the 1997 VH1 *Storytellers* broadcast, Adam discussed all of the misinterpretations of who (or what) "Mr. Jones" really was. In actuality, Mr. Jones is Marty Jones, friend and former band mate of Adam's. The two were in Sordid Humor and Himalayans together.

Adam says that Maria from "Round Here," essentially, is himself.

The girl in "Anna Begins" was an Australian girl that Adam met and fell in love with when he went backpacking on a Greek Island in 1989. She is married now but the two still talk occasionally.

Some of the inspiration for "Rain King" came from the book *Henderson the Rain King* by Saul Bellow, a book Adam read in college.

"Ghost Train" is the cornerstone of the "train" element found in some of Counting Crows' songs, such as "Goodnight Elisabeth" and "High Life." The trains represent falling in love and learning about a person and the consequences of staying on that "train."

The "sha-la-la"s in "Mr. Jones" were basically a joke to annoy Adam's friend and *August and Everything After* executive producer Gary Gersh. Because of this, Adam was frequently compared to Van Morrison.

"Round Here" was originally written by Himalayans, a Bay Area band that Adam was in prior to Counting Crows. If you look in the song credits, you will notice that the music is credited to Dave Jansuko, Dan Jewett, and Chris Roldan, all former Himalayans band members. The words, however, were written by Adam.

"A Murder of One" was originally named "Counting Crows."

The first known recording of "Mr. Jones" is a demo that was recorded in Adam's garage with a keyboard and drum machine.

An old English rhyme is quoted in the middle of "A Murder of One."

Several songs from *August and Everything After* exist on the band's original demo tape, now titled "Flying Demos." The songs are "Rain King," "Omaha," "Mr. Jones," "Anna Begins," and "Round Here." "Omaha" has a bit more upbeat sound and "Rain King" has a few extra lyrics.

"Sullivan Street" was probably written sometime in early 1992. During a May 28, 1992 concert, Adam called the song "fairly new."

III - Everything Else

The album was recorded in a house on a hill up Tigertail
Road above Brentwood in West Los Angeles, marking
the beginning of a "house on a hill" recording tradition
that Counting Crows have kept with them throughout the
album-making process. Robbie Robertson, guitarist for
The Band, turned Adam and Dave Bryson onto this idea
before they recorded *August and Everything After*. The
studio inside the house was set up for Counting Crows
for their first album, but they have since set it up themselves.

The lyrics for the song *August and Everything After* can be
found on the album cover. This song was never released
and it is said that copies exist only in the hands of
Counting Crows' record company and Adam's father. It
was rumored to be a hidden track on "Recovering the
Satellites" but the rumor proved to be false.

Maria McKee, who sang background vocals on *August and
Everything After*, most notably "Sullivan Street," has
several albums out, including "Life is Sweet," "You
Gotta Sin to be Saved," and "Maria McKee." She and
Adam did a duet on a song called "Opelousas (Sweet
Relief)" on a Victoria Williams benefit album titled
Sweet Relief.

Some members of Jayhawks, a Minneapolis, Minnesota
band, also did background vocals on the album.

The house in the "Mr. Jones" video is actually a replica.

Recovering the Satellites
Released 10-15-96

Produced by Gil Norton.

Songs: Catapult, Angels of the Silences, Daylight Fading, I'm Not Sleeping, Goodnight Elisabeth, Children in Bloom, Have You Seen Me Lately?, Miller's Angels, Another Horsedreamer's Blues, Recovering the Satellites, Monkey, Mercury, A Long December, Walkaways.

Singles: A Long December, Angels of the Silences, and Daylight Fading.

Music Videos: A Long December, Angels of the Silences, and Daylight Fading.

1 - The Charts

Album Chart debut: October 29, 1996 at #1.

Album Chart Peak: October 29, 1996 at #1.

Singles Chart Debuts: Angels of the Silences - October 12, 1996; A Long December - December 7, 1996; Daylight Fading - Failed to chart.

Singles Weeks on Chart: Angels of the Silences - 9; A Long December - 28.

Recovering the Satellites was certified double platinum in mid-1997.

11 - The Songs

"Catapult" originally began as a song about a girl, but a great deal of Adam's inspiration for the song came from the death of Kurt Cobain.

The girl, Elisabeth, mentioned in "Goodnight Elisabeth" is actually named Betsy.

"Children in Bloom" was written shortly before the band left for their *August and Everything After* tour. The "Nicole" mentioned in "Children in Bloom" is Adam's sister.

Both "Goodnight Elisabeth" and "Children in Bloom" were played during the *August and Everything After* tour.

"Miller's Angels" was recorded for the movie *The Crossing Guard* but it didn't make the final cut. It was recorded a week after Ben joined the band. On the lyrics page for "Miller's Angels," the song is noted as being "For Sean and me." Sean is Sean Penn, the director of *The Crossing Guard.*

Adam's adjustment period is reflected in many of the songs on *Recovering the Satellites*. The second half of the album deals with the issues of fame and coping, highlighted in such songs as "Have You Seen Me Lately?" and "Recovering the Satellites."

"Daylight Fading" originally had very different lyrics with only the chorus being similar to the track that appears on *Recovering the Satellites.*

Adam said that "Monkey" is the only positive love song that he has ever written.

The background vocals to "Monkey" are "Isn't it a shame/ Gone away again/And I've been in/Can't you see the pain I'm in/Monkey, where you been?"

In concert, Adam has been known to say about "Mercury," "This is not a song about love, this is a song about addiction." It is about being so wrapped up in a relationship even when you know the person you're in the relationship with is bad for you.

"Mercury" took only one day to be learned, rehearsed, and recorded.

One of Adam's friends was in a bad car wreck when Counting Crows were recording *Recovering the Satellites.* Adam wrote the song in his head when he was at the hospital visiting his friend. He then went back to house where the band was recording and "A Long December" was recorded during the early hours of the morning. The version that appears on the album was only the sixth take.

"Hillside Manor," mentioned in "A Long December," is actually a small house in Hollywood Hills where a few of Adam's friends live. He went to talk to them late in the night after visiting the hospital to see his friend.

Some of the inspiration for "Another Horsedreamer's Blues" came from the play "Geography of a Horse Dreamer" by Sam Shepard.

III - Everything Else

This album was also recorded in a big house on a hill, this time in Hollywood. VH1 broadcast a one-hour special on *Recovering the Satellites* with footage from inside the house.

It took six months to write *Recovering the Satellites* and the first half of 1996 to record it.

Two songs, "Good Luck" and "Chelsea," were recorded for *Recovering the Satellites* but didn't end up on the album because they didn't fit with the theme.

The typed song on the piano behind the "Walkaways" lyrics is "Chelsea."

"Margery Dreams of Horses" was also supposed to be on *Recovering the Satellites*. Although an extremely old song that dates back to the band's demo days, Adam introduced it during a great deal of the *August and Everything After* tour as "a song from our new album." However, it was not included because Adam felt it didn't fit the time range or the theme of the album.

Zippo lighters were used at the beginning of "Goodnight Elisabeth." Ben had the honor of clicking them.

Ben once again had the honor of "playing" light bulbs during "I'm Not Sleeping." The sound was created by drumming them on a concrete floor until they broke.

A video was recorded for "Catapult" January 18 and 19, 1997, but it was not used.

Courteney Cox appears in the "A Long December" video.

The drawing that appears under the CD in *Recovering the Satellites* was drawn by Matt. He was mad at everyone one night and started doodling. The band thought it was so funny that they kept the drawing up for the remainder of the recording process. It is actually a self-portrait but everyone thought it looked like Adam because Matt forgot to draw his goatee.

It's a beautiful feeling to experience a new Counting Crows song. You hang on every new word and let every new sound tug at your every emotion. It's crisp and new yet somehow wholly familiar. Even when the memories of the first listen begin to fade and the song ages, there still seems to be some tiny piece of the song that remains untouched and new. Perhaps every Counting Crows fan is searching for that untouched and new piece.

Across a Wire
Released 7-14-98

Full album title: *Across A Wire: Live in New York*

Songs: Disc 1 - Round Here, Have You Seen Me Lately?, Angels of the Silences, Catapult, Mr. Jones, Rain King, Mercury, Ghost Train, Anna Begins, and Chelsea (hidden track). Disc 2 - Recovering the Satellites, Angels of the Silences, Rain King, Sullivan Street, Children in Bloom, Have You Seen Me Lately?, Raining in Baltimore, Round Here, I'm Not Sleeping, A Murder of One, A Long December, Walkaways.

The first disc was recorded on August 12, 1997 for VH1 Storytellers and the second disc was recorded on November 6, 1997 for MTV Live From the 10 Spot.

This double CD live set was released in an effort to hold over fans until the new album, *This Desert Life*, was released.

1 - The Charts

Across A Wire has sold slightly over 280,000 copies.

11 - The Songs

The first disc holds a hidden track. The song, "Chelsea," was recorded for *Recovering the Satellites* but didn't make the cut. The horns in the song were played by several members of Soul Rebels, a band from New Orleans. Curtis Watson played trumpet, William Terry played saxophone, and Steven "Coolbone" Johnson played trombone.

The track listings of the discs vary slightly from the original VH1 and MTV aired broadcasts. The Storytellers disc is missing "A Long December," whereas the Live From the 10 Spot disc is missing "Goodnight Elisabeth," "Catapult," "Mr. Jones," "Omaha," and "Anna Begins." The additional, unaired tracks on the Storytellers disc are "Round Here," "Mercury," and "Anna Begins." The unaired tracks on the Live From the 10 Spot disc are "Children in Bloom" "Raining in Baltimore," and "Wiseblood" (cover song).

4
This Desert Life
Released 11-2-99

Produced by David Lowery (lead singer for Cracker) and
   Dennis Herring.

Songs: Hanginaround, Mrs. Potter's Lullaby, Amy Hit the
   Atmosphere, Four Days, All My Friends, High Life,
   Colorblind, I Wish I Was a Girl, Speedway, St. Robinson
   In His Cadillac Dream, and Kid Things (hidden track).

Singles: Hanginaround, Mrs. Potter's Lullaby (released in
   two parts), and All My Friends. *As of September 2000.

Music Videos: Hanginaround (Released October 4), Mrs.
   Potter's Lullaby, and All My Friends.

1 - The Charts

Album Chart debut: November 16, 1999 at #8.

Album Chart Peak: November 16, 1999 at #8.

"Hanginaround" debuted on the Billboard 100 charts at #29.

This Desert Life sold 129,000 copies in the first week. It was
   certified platinum on January 24, 2000.

II - The Songs

"Mrs. Potter" is actually the actress Monica Potter. She appeared on the television show *The Young and the Restless* and in movies such as *Con Air* and *Patch Adams*.

The songs "Mrs. Potter's Lullaby," "Four Days," "Color-blind," and "Kid Things" are known as "the Ohio songs" since Monica Potter is from Ohio.

"Mrs. Potter's Lullaby" was written after Adam saw a movie that Monica Potter was in. He said it was another one of his "actress infatuations." He didn't know exactly what to write about so he wrote the song as if he were telling her about his life and the things that had been running through his head in the recent weeks. A friend of Adam's introduced him to Monica and they went out to dinner. After that, Monica went back to the recording studio and listened to the band record the song. Dennis Herring gave her a copy of the song before she left. After many weeks of going nowhere with the song, Adam listened to the cassette Monica had and loved it. With some minor editing, that take landed on the album.

"Four Days" was written after Adam hadn't heard from Monica for four days and nights. She had left for Ohio to visit family and he didn't want to call her answering machine repeatedly.

"Colorblind" is about desperately wanting someone to pull all of the emotions out of you. It was written after Monica had already left town, shortly before "Four Days" was written.

"Kid Things" (the hidden track) was written when Adam finally did hear from Monica and they sat up all night on the phone. He compared it to being sixteen years old again and talking on the phone to the person you like for hours and hours.

"Amy Hit the Atmosphere" is about a friend of Adam's who moved from Montana to Hollywood. She was a ballerina but she fell in with the wrong group of people and became a junkie. She eventually got clean, moved back to Montana, and became a ballerina again.

"Mrs. Potter's Lullaby," "Amy Hit the Atmosphere," "Four Days," and "Kid Things" are basically live tracks with little or no overdubbing.

"Colorblind" was featured in the movie "Cruel Intentions."

Dave Bryson said that they attempted to distort the sound in "Kid Things" as much as possible. They used micro cassette recorders and $10 microphones.

"Speedway" is a sequel to "Mercury." It's about trying to get out of the bad, addicting, relationship with the girl described in "Mercury."

Before "Speedway" had a title, Ben called it "I'm Outta Here, You Bitch."

"I Wish I Was a Girl" is about the girlfriend, Elisabeth, Adam had before he left for the *August and Everything After* tour. She thought he was cheating on her although he wasn't. "I Wish I Was a Girl" revolves around the trust issue in relationships.

"Hanginaround" is about Adam's experience with growing up in Berkeley, smoking weed, and basically going nowhere with his life. Although one of the most "live" sounding tracks on the album, it is actually the song with the most overdubs and layered sounds. There are two types of background vocals — drunken and sober. The drunken background vocals were recorded by David Lowery, Ben, Adam, and Dan one night, along with a few handclaps. They liked how the handclaps sounded, so they invited a bunch of their friends over the next day to clap along and sing more background vocals. All of the handclaps are credited in the liner notes.

The music in "Hanginaround" was partially inspired by the song "Steal My Sunshine" by the band Len. Adam met Len before they had a record deal.

"Hanginaround" it was originally named "Bummin' Around."

"High Life" is about looking back on your life and trying to decide if you're really in the place you want to be. It also mentions the "train element," alluding to the first line in "Goodnight Elisabeth."

The name of the album comes from a line in "High Life" that mentions "this desert life."

Adam has said that "All My Friends" is a song about reflecting upon your life and seeing all of your "friends and lovers" growing up and starting their lives. It's also about getting on with your life with or without your friends and family.

According to the reference of being thirty-three in "All My Friends," the song should have been written between August 1, 1997 and August 1, 1998.

III - Everything Else

Two songs that were written for *This Desert Life* but do not appear on the album are "Sundays" and "She Don't Want Nobody Near." Both of these songs were performed at the Viper Room in Los Angeles in April 1998.

The album cover and interior illustrations are by Dave McKean. It is very similar to the cover of the book *The Day I Swapped My Dad For Two Goldfish*, also illustrated by Dave McKean.

The first printing of the album cover contains an error. On the outside track listing, "Cadillac" in "St. Robinson In His Cadillac Dream" is misspelled "Cadallac."

The second single was supposed to be "St. Robinson In His Cadillac Dream," but it was changed to "Mrs. Potter's Lullaby." It's the second time "St. Robinson" was booted — it almost replaced "Hanginaround" as the first single.

In the "Hanginaround" video, the man in the bus who looks up and smiles is Tom Mullally, Counting Crows' tour manager. The girl at the end of the video at the bus stop is Amy Smart. She was in the movie *Varsity Blues*.

The video for "Hanginaround" was shot both in Adam's living room and in Echo Park. Many of the band members from Joe 90, Gigolo Aunts, and Remy Zero are in the living room scene (which is, in fact, really Adam's living room).

Adam played a xylophone for *This Desert Life*, mostly to have fun while he was bored in the vocal booth. However, it worked out and they used the it on certain songs.

Under the "Speedway" lyrics, there is a photograph of Holloway Drive. In Los Angeles, Holloway Drive forms an intersection with North La Cienega Boulevard, the street on which Counting Crows' management, Direct Management Group Inc., is located.

They finished mixing *This Desert Life* the week of February 7, 1999.

Dave Gibbs of Gigolo Aunts has a cameo in the video for "Mrs. Potter's Lullaby." He is seen in the first party scene wearing a jean jacket and holding a bottle of water.

The video for "Mrs. Potter's Lullaby" was rarely shown due to its length. Most fans saw it for the first time when it was encoded on Quicktime.com.

5
Singles, Imports
& Compilations

1 - Singles

Counting Crows do not release singles within the United States. All singles are either UK or Australia imports.

- "Rain King" - Contains "Rain King," "Anna Begins" (live), and "Round Here" (live).

- "Round Here" - Contains "Round Here," "Ghost Train," and "The Ghost In You" (live and unreleased).

- "Mr. Jones" - Contains "Mr. Jones," "Raining in Baltimore," "Mr. Jones" (live and acoustic), and "Rain King" (live and acoustic).

- "Omaha" - "Omaha," "Anna Begins" (live), and "Round Here" (live).

- "Angels of the Silences" - "Angels of the Silences," "Recovering the Satellites," and "Round Here" (live).

- "A Long December" - "A Long December," "Ghost Train" (live) and "Sullivan Street" (live).

- "Daylight Fading" Part 1 - "Daylight Fading," "Time and Time Again" (live) and "Miller's Angels" (demo).

- "Daylight Fading Part 2 - "Daylight Fading," "Rain King" (live), and "Daylight Fading" (live).

- "Hanginaround" Part 1 - "Hanginaround," "Mercury"(live), and "Goodnight Elisabeth" (live).

- "Hanginaround" Part 2 - "Hanginaround," "Baby, I'm a Big Star Now," and "Omaha" (live).

II - Imports

- "Daylight Fading" Interactive CD - Australia
Contains "Daylight Fading," "Rain King" (live), "Time and Time Again" (live), "Miller's Angels" (demo), and an interactive program for your computer.

- *Maximum Counting Crows*
Not officially endorsed. Contains band interviews (on CD), an eight-page informational booklet, and a poster.

III - Compilations

- *Best of Mountain Stage,* Volume 7 - "Mr. Jones"

- *DGC Rarities*, Volume 1 - "Einstein On the Beach (For An Eggman)"

- *MTV Buzz Bin*, Volume 2 - "Mr. Jones"

- *MTV First 1000 Years: Rock* - "Mr. Jones"

- *Music For Our Mother Earth*, Volume 2 - "Angels of the Silences"

- *Saturday Night Live 25*, Volume 1 - "Round Here"

- *Best of VH1 Storytellers*, Volume 1 - "Rain King"

IV - Other Releases

- *By The Time We Got To Woodstock* - Limited to 1,000 copies. Official bootleg. Contains "Mr. Jones," "Angels of the Silences," "Recovering the Satellites," "Have You Seen Me Lately?," "Daylight Fading," "Mercury," "Omaha," "Round Here," "Rain King," "A Murder of One," "Goodnight Elisabeth," "A Long December," and "Anna Begins" (all live).

- *Face the Promised Land* - Limited to 5,000 copies. Official bootleg. "Mr. Jones," "Angels of the Silences," "I Wish I Was a Girl," "High Life," "Omaha," "Monkey," "All My Friends," "Four Days," "St. Robinson in His Cadillac Dream," "Rain King," "Hanginaround," "Kid Things," "A Long December," and "Walkaways." (Recorded live at Magness Arena in Denver, Colorado, on December 2, 1999.)

- Live At The Fox Theatre - Special promotion with Best Buy when *This Desert Life* was released. Limited copies. Contains "Mercury," "Omaha," "Another Horsedreamer's Blues," and "Goodnight Elisabeth."

- *Clueless* soundtrack - "The Ghost In You"

- *Cruel Intentions* soundtrack - "Colorblind"

- *August and Everything After, Recovering the Satellites,* and *This Desert Life* have been released on vinyl.

- *August and Everything After* and *Recovering the Satellites* have been released on special 24K gold discs.

6
Band Members on
Other Albums

1 - Adam Duritz

- The Wallflowers, *Bringing Down the Horse*: Background vocals on "Sixth Avenue Heartache."

- Sordid Humor, *Light Music For Dying People*: Back-up vocals on "Iceland," "Doris Day," "Gun Man," "Barbarossa," "Lolita," "Ben and Mary," "Miami Beach," "Hat Song," "Helena," and "Go Away."

- Gigolo Aunts, *Minor Chords and Major Themes*: Background vocals on "The Big Lie."

- Nanci Griffith, *Flyer*: Co-wrote and dueted on "Going Back to Georgia." Harmony vocals on "Nobody's Angel" and "Talk To Me While I'm Listening."

- Joe 90, *Dream This* - Counter melodies on "Drive" and "Ferris Wheel."

- Dogs Eye View, *Daisy* - Background vocals on "Last Letter Home" and "Homecoming Parade."

- Various Artists, *I-10 Chronicles* - Contributed a cover of "Carmelita," a song by Warren Zevon. David Immergluck and David Hidalgo from Los Lobos also played on the song.

- Peter Stuart, *Songs About You* - Background vocals on "Propeller Girl" from the EP and several other songs on the full album.

II - Dave Bryson

- Sordid Humor, *Light Music for Dying People*: Produced and engineered "Iceland," "Doris Day," "Barbarossa," "Miami Beach," "Hat Song," "Helena," and "Go Away." Provided the ghost voices on "Doris Day."

- Sordid Humor, *Tony Don't*: He mixed the entire EP. It includes "Jumpin' Jesus," a song that Counting Crows have covered in the past.

- Faith No More, *Angel Dust*: Co-mixed the album with Matt Wallace.

- Mr. Henry, *40 Watt Fade*: Recorded, produced, and mixed the entire album.

- Train, *Train*: Mixed the entire album except for "If You Leave."

- Recorded demos for Dog's Eye View, Seven Day Diary, Monks of Doom, and Cola.

III - Charlie Gillingham

- Train, *Train*: Played organ, melotron, and piano.

- Cola, *Whatnot*: Played Hammond organ on "Bike Racks," "Chastity's Cross," "Prozac," "Perforated

Heart," and "Gasoline;" played Mellotron on "Fun;" played cello sample on "Gasoline;" played horn sample on "Shotgun'" and piano "noise" on "Gasoline."

- Cracker, *The Golden Age* - Played organ on "I Hate My Generation" and "Dixie Babylon."

- American Music Club, *United Kingdom*: Played piano.

- Jerry Schelfer, *Slipaway*: Played piano and organ (Hammond).

- Wire Train, *Point Break soundtrack*: Played on the song "I Will Not Fall."

- Various Artists, *Acoustic Music Project*: Played piano and accordion on most songs.

IV - Ben Mize

- Jars of Clay, *If I Left the Zoo*: Played drums on the entire album.

- Marlee MacLeod, *Drive Too Fast*: Played drums on the album.

It's funny how a song will make you look at things in a different light. It's hard not to think of "Anna Begins" when you're falling in love or "A Long December" when the winter is slowing you down or "Colorblind" when you're wishing desperately that someone would understand you. Songs stay with you forever.

Section
Three

LIVE
PERFORMANCES

It's a moment that no Counting Crows fan will ever forget: the moment when you look up and you swear that Adam's looking right in your eyes or Dan's playing just for you. It's like you have suddenly hit something you've gravitated towards for years. There's nothing quite like that feeling.

1
Live
Versions

Counting Crows have been recognized as an extremely talented live band. They tend to improvise many of their songs, most notably songs from *August and Everything After* such as "Round Here" and "Rain King." In addition to improvising, Counting Crows have performed several unreleased songs at shows in the past. However, the more albums that they have, the less unreleased material they play.

1 - *August...* - Live

The most improvised Counting Crows song ever, "Round Here," is from *August and Everything After*. Many fans consider it the pinnacle of a Counting Crows live performance. Because of how important it is to live Counting Crows shows and the amount of information that exists about live versions, Chapter Two is dedicated to "Round Here."

If asked to describe a live performance of "Omaha," many fans would probably point out Charlie's red accordion. He is known for climbing atop speakers during this song, especially during the opening notes.

"Mr. Jones" has gone through a metamorphosis throughout its life as a live song. Although a decidedly electric song on *August and Everything After*, it began to take on a slower pace as the *August and Everything After* touring progressed. By the time the *Recovering the Satellites* tour began, it was completely acoustic, soon being preceded by several lines of The Byrds' "So You Wanna Be a Rock n' Roll Star." Beginning with the summer 1999 pre-*This Desert Life* tour, the song went back to its full electric glory, although it usually started off with a few acoustic lines.

The line "I want to be Bob Dylan" from "Mr. Jones" has been changed on several occasions. Adam has also said "Alex Chilton" (the lead singer of Big Star), "David Lowery" (the lead singer of Cracker) and "Jakob Dylan" (when touring with Jakob's band The Wallflowers). He has said "blue guitar" instead of "gray guitar" on a few occasions.

"Perfect Blue Buildings" was played frequently during the *August and Everything After* tour, but rarely during the *Recovering the Satellites* or *This Desert Life* tours.

"Rain King" is also another heavily improvised song, although not nearly as much as "Round Here." It has been through many sound transformations, including electric, acoustic, and somewhere in-between. Adam has been known to mention Elisabeth in live versions of this song, usually in a line declaring his apologies to her.

"Raining in Baltimore" had almost never been played live until a girl begged Adam at the July 15, 1997 Hershey, Pennsylvania show to play it. He did, and they played it at nearly every show the rest of 1997.

"A Murder of One" is now a very electric song. Adam usually jumps up and down during the song and screams at the audience to "Get the hell up!" He often sings, "I have been to Paris, I have been to Rome, I have gone to

London and I am all alone," sometimes replacing "London" with the city that he is currently in. He has been known to change the last few words to "and I am not alone."

Every song on *August and Everything After* has been played acoustically at one point.

Both "Round Here" and "Mr. Jones" have been played on late-night television shows.

11 - *Recovering...* - Live

"Daylight Fading" originally had strikingly different lyrics. This song, with its original lyrics, was first played in 1995 at the Viper Room in Los Angeles.

Starting in late 1999, Adam began adding a lyric about "waiting for the telephone" in place of a lot of the "la-la's" in the middle of "Daylight Fading."

When "I'm Not Sleeping" was first played at the Hollywood Grand on November 16, 1995, a few of the lyrics in the middle were slightly different.

Fans have been known to hold up lighters during Matt's bass solo in "Children in Bloom."

Although very few songs from *Recovering the Satellites* are improvised much or at all, "Mercury" began being improvised both musically and lyrically a great deal during the pre-*This Desert Life* and *This Desert Life* tours. Adam began telling stories about the song and the girl in the song, sometimes repeating over and over again, "This is not a song about love, this is a song about addiction." David Immergluck's electric slide guitar added a fantastic element to the song which had not been included in the song since the original recording.

Starting with the summer 1999 pre-*This Desert Life* tour, David Immergluck began playing the guitar during "Another Horsedreamer's Blues," replacing the music Adam usually played on the Wurlitzer.

During the *Recovering the Satellites* tour, they almost always opened up with "Recovering the Satellites," fittingly.

"A Long December" has been improvised musically since the middle of the *Recovering the Satellites* tour, with a long accordion intro. However, it was not improvised lyrically until November 1999 when Adam began adding lyrics to the beginning over a piano solo. He has not been adding lyrics at every concert but the piano solo has replaced the accordion solo.

"Walkaways" has become the expected last song of the encore since the release of *Recovering the Satellites*. It has appeared in different places in the set list (most notably first in Boston on October 31, 1999, obviously due to the fact that Boston is mentioned in the lyrics) but it is generally played last.

Two songs from *Recovering the Satellites* have been played live since the *August and Everything After* tour. "Goodnight Elisabeth" was played as early as January 1994 and "Children in Bloom" as early as September 1993 (the same month that *August and Everything After* was released).

"Recovering the Satellites," "Angels of the Silences," and "Daylight Fading" were the most-played songs from *Recovering the Satellites* during the *Recovering the Satellites* tour.

The least-played *Recovering the Satellites* song is "Miller's Angels." "Monkey" was played, although not that much. Starting with the *This Desert Life* tour, the band began performing it almost every night.

"Catapult," "Angels of the Silences," and "Have You Seen Me Lately?" have been played acoustically.

"Catapult," "Daylight Fading," and "A Long December" have been played on late-night television shows.

"California Dreamin'" by the Mamas and the Papas was played before every *Recovering the Satellites* tour show.

III - *Desert...* - Live

In concert, "Hanginaround" is highlighted with Counting Crows and all of the opening bands going onstage, clapping, dancing, and singing. Many people describe it as looking like a big party. Adam instructs everyone in the audience to clap along.

During "Colorblind," Ben gets up from his drum set and plays a xylophone to Adam's left. Matt plays piano.

During the summer 1999 pre-*This Desert Life* tour, "Hanginaround," "Mrs. Potter's Lullaby," "Four Days," "Speedway," "St. Robinson In His Cadillac Dream," and "Kid Things" were played live, usually averaging two to three new songs per show.

"Four Days" was first played at the July 16, 1999 Toledo, Ohio song. Since it mentions Ohio, Adam said, "We weren't going to play this song tonight, but it occurred to me we kind of have to."

Matt plays guitar during "Four Days."

"St. Robinson In His Cadillac Dream" was first played live at the Viper Room on April 19, 1998.

Charlie plays an acoustic guitar during "Kid Things."

During the pre-*This Desert Life* tour, Adam said that they recorded "Kid Things" for the album but didn't end up putting it on. They did — just not in the official song listing.

The most-played songs from *This Desert Life* seem to be "Hanginaround" and "St. Robinson In His Cadillac Dream."

Several songs were played before *This Desert Life* shows. They are: "Magical Mystery Tour" by the Beatles (the most popular), "Whippin' Picadilly" by Gomez, and "Abide Me" by Thelonius Monk. The shows always ends with "There She Goes Again" by The La's.

"Hanginaround" and "Kid Things" have been played on late-night television shows. "Hanginaround" has been played twice — once with Joe 90 and Gigolo Aunts (tour mates at the time) and once without.

IV - Quoted Songs

During his improvs, Adam has quoted a great deal of songs over the years. Here's a listing of quite a few of them.

• "Thunder Road" by Bruce Springsteen - "Rain King" and "Round Here"

• "Private Archipelago" by Sordid Humor - "Round Here"

- "So You Want To Be A Rock n' Roll Star" by The Byrds - "Round Here" and "Mr. Jones"

- "Doris Day" by Sordid Humor - "Round Here" and "A Murder of One"

- "At the Zoo" by Simon and Garfunkel - "Mr. Jones"

- "Just Like Tom Thumb's Blues" by Bob Dylan - "A Murder of One"

- "September Gurls" by Big Star - "Rain King"

- "Sometimes It Snows In April" by Prince - "Perfect Blue Buildings"

- "Eleanor Rigby" by the Beatles - "A Murder of One" and "Round Here"

- "Girl From the North Country" by Bob Dylan - "Time and Time Again"

- "Radiation Vibe" by Fountains of Wayne - "Round Here"

- "Red Hill Mining Town" by U2 - "A Murder of One"

- "No Scrubs" by TLC - "Hanginaround"

- "She Doesn't Exist Anymore" by Robyn Hitchcock - "Round Here"

- "Live Forever" by Oasis - "A Long December"

- "Positively Fourth Street" by Bob Dylan - "Round Here"

V - "A Long December"

During the summer 1999 pre-*This Desert Life* tour, Adam introduced "A Long December" as several different songs. They were:

- "Benny and the Jets" - Elton John
- "Cold As Ice" - "Foreigner"
- "Bohemian Rhapsody" - Queen
- "Beth" - Kiss

They actually did begin to play "Cold As Ice" on several occasions but stopped before completing the first few lines.

2
"Round Here"

"Round Here" is the most improvised live Counting Crows song. It is played at almost every concert (although its play became somewhat rare during the last half of the *This Desert Life* tour) and versions range from five or six minutes to over thirteen minutes in length.

Although it is one of the most popular Counting Crows songs, it is not an entirely Crows song. It was written by Himalayans, a previous band of Adam's. The words are Adam's, but the music is credited to three of Adam's Himalayans band mates and Dave Bryson. The original version is faster in many parts and a few lyrics are slightly different. The original lyrics mention a warehouse rather than a house, undoubtedly the warehouse Adam and Dave Immergluck lived in while trying to make it in the music business.

1 - Past Improvs

There are so many different improvs for this song, it would be impossible to even attempt to name them all. However, here are a few of the more popular ones. Keep in mind that within all of these improvs, there are many different versions. Improvs tend to start on a whim one night and then become more developed as the nights and shows go by.

- "Catch me if I was falling, kiss me if I was leaving, hold me if I was lonely." - This is an older improv that was used a lot in the *August and Everything After* tour days. Sometimes it was posed as a question and at other times it was a plea or perhaps even a demand. It was usually tacked on at the very end, unlike some improvs that occur right in the middle of the song. A beautiful rendition of this improv exists in the 1994 performance on the David Letterman Show.

- "One more time through the mill." - This is also an older improv but it has been used as late as 1997. It is a very bitter improv where Adam repeatedly says how it has been "one more time through the mill" and sometimes sings about being a "cheap fucking thrill."

- "Green sky/Blue sky/Gray sky" - This is a very popular improv that has been changed over the past few years with many existing versions. Adam usually says something about having a sky in his head or heart, or he says something about locking the sky away. It is sometimes coupled with a bit about a sun that has stopped spinning around.

- "Did you think that you were dreaming?" - Anyone who has watched the 1997 MTV Live From the 10 Spot performance can probably remember this version. Adam sat at the edge of the stage and asked this question several times, ending with the answer that sometimes he doesn't know.

- "It's all right." - This is a slightly newer improv from October or November 1999. It usually consists of Adam repeating over and over again that "it's all right" or "it will be all right."

- "The story" - Adam sometimes tells a story before "Round Here" about the time when he and Dave Immergluck were living in a warehouse in Berkeley and trying to make it as musicians. He usually talks about the warehouse they lived in being on 4th Street, 3rd Street being railroad tracks, 2nd Street being a dirt road, 1st Street being the freeway, and beyond that being San Francisco Bay. Sometimes he talks about working all day, playing all night, and wondering if they were ever going to make it as a band. It tends to be an inspirational talk in addition to a story.

II - Quoted Songs

Adam quotes several songs during "Round Here." They are:

- "Private Archipelago" by Sordid Humor
- "So You Want To Be A Rock n' Roll Star" by The Byrds
- "Doris Day" by Sordid Humor
- "Eleanor Rigby" by the Beatles
- "Radiation Vibe" by Fountains of Wayne
- "She Doesn't Exist Anymore" by Robyn Hitchcock

Several Counting Crows songs have also been quoted in the middle of "Round Here." They are:

- "Have You Seen Me Lately?"
- "Mrs. Potter's Lullaby"
- "Miller's Angels"
- "Goodnight Elisabeth"
- "Barely Out of Tuesday" (unreleased)
- "Shallow Days" (unreleased)
- "Here Comes That Feeling Again" (unreleased)

III - Random Lengths

- 5 minutes, 4 seconds - May 16, 1992; San Francisco, California; Slim's Nightclub

- 5 minutes, 11 seconds - October 6, 1993; Dallas, Texas; Deep Ellum Live

- 5 minutes, 14 seconds - February 16, 1994; Montreal, Canada; Club Soda

- 8 minutes, 21 seconds - November 15, 1994; London, England; Shepard's Bush Empire

- 8 minutes, 52 seconds - November 16, 1995; Holly-wood, California; Hollywood Grand

- 9 minutes, 20 seconds - November 6, 1997; New York, NY; Hammerstein Ballroom

- 9 minutes, 26 seconds - July 24, 1999; Rome, New York; Woodstock

- 10 minutes, 26 seconds - December 17, 1996; Los Angeles, California; Wiltern Theater

- 10 minutes, 33 seconds - September 8, 1996; Holly-wood, California; John Anson Ford Theater

- 12 minutes, 30 seconds - July 19, 1999; Sea Bright, New Jersey; Tradewinds

- 13 minutes, 3 seconds - November 19, 1999; Columbus, Ohio; Veteran's Memorial

- 10 minutes, 5 seconds - June 26, 2000; Paris, France; Elysee Montmartre

3
Notable
Shows

At a November 7, 1993 radio show (Idiot's Delight in New York, NY), Steve Bowman played a cardboard box rather than a drum set.

On December 2, 1996 at a New York City show, Adam jumped the wrong way and injured his knee. He continued the show but took a one-song break to get his knee wrapped. During this break, Dan sang "Wiseblood" (a cover song).

In December 1996, Counting Crows played The Late Show With David Letterman an unprecedented two nights in a row. On the 11th of December, they played "Catapult." They returned the next night at David Letterman's request and played "A Long December."

On August 1, 1997, a Baltimore radio station broadcasted a Counting Crows show live from the Merriweather Post Pavilion in Columbia, Maryland. Since it was Adam's birthday, there was, of course, a celebration. In the middle of their set, two women in bikinis came out onstage and sang "Happy Birthday" to Adam. Near the end of the set during "A Long December," Adam started laughing in the middle of the song because cake was being thrown at him.

The next month at a Concord Pavilion, Concord, California show, Adam had to restart "Raining in Baltimore" because a person dressed as Barney came out onstage.

Although not a Counting Crows show, the February 20, 1998 Seattle, Washington, Matchbox 20 show contained a surprising element — Adam. He dueted with Rob Thomas during "Mamas Don't Let Their Babies Grow Up to Be Cowboys" and "Long Day." At the June 15, 2000 London, England Matchbox 20 show, Adam and Charlie guested on "Mamas Don't Let Their Babies Grow Up to Be Cowboys" yet again.

The entire Halloween 1999 show in Boston was a very festive one. Counting Crows and both opening bands — Joe 90 and Gigolo Aunts — dressed for the occasion. Adam dressed up as bunny, Charlie went as Elvis, Matt was Yoda, David Immergluck was the devil, David Bryson was a soldier, Dan was Jughead, and Ben was a forest ranger. They stayed in-costume the entire show.

"Here Comes That Feeling Again," written for an independent film, was first played at a Kalamazoo, Michigan show on May 28, 2000. The song was recorded in Chicago over the next two days.

"My Love" was first played in East Lansing, Michigan, on May 31, 2000. Both this song and "Here Comes That Feeling Again" were written for the independent film "Rope Walk," directed by Matt Brown.

Adam has played two "secret shows" at the Shim Sham Club in New Orleans during the Jazz Fest. The first, in 1999, was with several of his musical friends and the second, in 2000, was with David Immergluck. Both shows started late at night and didn't end until the early morning hours. The sets mostly consisted of acoustic cover songs and a few Counting Crows songs, some of which were new.

4
Unreleased and
Cover Songs

1 - Unreleased Songs

The following songs were all written by Counting Crows but were never put on an official release.

- "A Greening of America"
- "A Mona Lisa"
- "40 Years"
- "Margery Dreams of Horses"
- "Good Luck"
- "Open All Night"
- "Barely Out of Tuesday"
- "Sundays"
- "She Don't Want Nobody Near"
- "Shallow Days"
- "Bulldog"
- "Lightning"
- "Suffocate"
- "Love and Addiction"
- "August and Everything After"
- "Closer to You"
- "Here Comes That Feeling Again"
- "My Love"

11 - Cover Songs

All of these songs have been played in concert by Counting Crows. This list does not include cover songs played during the acoustic Shim Sham shows which included quite a few cover songs.

- "This Must Be the Place" - Talking Heads
- "We're Only Love" - Mr. Dog
- "Maggie Mae" - Rod Stewart
- "Four White Stallions" - Patrick Winningham and Jeff Trott
- "The Ghost In You" - Psychadelic Furs
- "Caravan" - Van Morrison
- "Richest Man" - Bob Carter
- "Return of the Grievous Angel" - Gram Parsons
- "Sweet Home Alabama" - Lynyrd Skynyrd
- "A Good Year For the Roses" - George Jones
- "Jumpin' Jesus" - Sordid Humor
- "Six Different Ways" - The Cure
- "Wiseblood" - Kurt Stevenson
- "So You Wanna Be a Rock n' Roll Star" - The Byrds
- "Atlantic City" - Bruce Springsteen
- "Mercy" - Kurt Stevenson, Patrick Winningham, and Chris Boesel

5
Tour
Mates

Counting Crows have toured with many talented artists over the years. They have said that they like to tour with bands that *they* enjoy so that they can also enjoy a show every single night. Members of the band, especially Adam, have been known to sit out in the audience while the opening bands are playing. Below you will find a listing of those bands and some of the approximate tour dates.

- Cracker - Counting Crows opened for Cracker early November 1993 through mid-December 1993 and again late February 1994 through March 1994. Cracker opened for Counting Crows November 1994 through early December 1994 and again in late May 2000.

- Fiona Apple - She opened for Counting Crows during a few dates between late January 1997 and February 1997.

- Engine 88 - They were an opening band for several dates after Fiona Apple until early April 1997.

- Cake - Cake opened at several shows in May 1997 in Europe and November 1996 in the U.S.

- The Wallflowers - They were major tour mates during 1997. The Wallflowers opened at many shows from July until late September 1997.

- Gigolo Aunts - They have played with Counting Crows on many occasions. They played with Counting Crows and The Cranberries in November 1993 and at a show opening for Big Star with Counting Crows (as "The Shatners") in 1994. They opened at several Counting Crows and Wallflowers shows in September 1997. Gigolo Aunts toured again with Counting Crows, being the only opening band during the entire summer 1999 (July 6 - July 22) pre-*This Desert Life* tour. Shortly after that, they toured from October 26, 1999 until mid-December 1999 with Counting Crows and Joe 90.

- That Dog - They opened for Counting Crows and The Wallflowers at a few shows in August 1997.

- Suede and The Cranberries - Counting Crows' first full tour was an opening slot for these two bands. Suede was the headlining band.

- Lisa Loeb - She opened for their entire R*ecovering the Satellites* European leg.

- Paula Cole, Cox Family, Ben Folds Five, and Engine 88 - Counting Crows have done entire legs of tours with all four of these bands.

- Dog's Eye View - They were the opening act for Counting Crows from late October until early November 1997. They also played four opening dates in New York City during September 1994 with several other bands. Peter Stuart, their lead singer, opened on several tours. He played the second stage at the East Coast dates during late 2000 tour with Live.

- Neilson Hubbard - He opened at several dates in August and September 1997.

- Bettie Serveert - Another opening band for Counting Crows and The Wallflowers, performing at several dates in the summer 1997 tour. The also did nearly the entire November and December 1997 European tour, minus The Wallflowers. They played some October opening dates during the late 2000 tour with Live.

- The Usual - They opened for Counting Crows during their August 1999 South African tour dates.

- Joe 90 - They opened for Counting Crows with Gigolo Aunts (on most dates) from October 26, 1999 until February 3, 2000.

- Arid - The opening band during Counting Crows' February, March, and early April 2000 European tour.

- Live - They co-headlined with Counting Crows from late July 2000 through October 2000.

- Galactic, Unified Theory, The Negro Problem, and Verbow - All of these bands were opening acts in this order at various shows during the late 2000 tour with Live.

- There are quite a few performers that Counting Crows have done a few shows with but not a long tour. They include Maria McKee, Midnight Oil, Sneetches, Third Eye Blind, Wade, 10Basst, Train, Remy Zero, Alex Chilton, eight opening performances for Rolling Stones, Mr. Henry (on a second stage) and Kieran Kennedy.

Some of the preceding artists' albums:

Joe 90 - *Dream This*

Gigolo Aunts - *Minor Chords and Major Themes, Learn to Play Guitar, Flippin' Out, Full-On Bloom, Tales From the Vinegar Side*

Cracker - *Cracker Brand, Kerosene Hat, The Golden Age, Gentlemen's Blues, Garage d'Or*

Cake - *Motorcade of Generosity, Fashion Nugget, Prolonging the Magic*

Remy Zero - *Chloroform Days, Remy Zero, Villa Elaine*

Neilson Hubbard - *Say Something Warm, Holding Flowers, Consolation Prize, The Slide Project*

Bettie Serveert - *Dust Bunnies, Lamprey*

Arid - *Little Things of Venom, At the Close of Every Day*

Live - *Mental Jewelry, Throwing Copper, Secret Samadhi, The Distance to Here*

Dog's Eye View - *Happy Nowhere, Daisy*

Galactic - *Coolin' Off, Crazyhorse Mongoose, Late for the Future*

6
Television
Appearances

- January 15, 1994 - Saturday Night Live. "Round Here" and "Mr. Jones."

- March 31, 1994 - The Late Show With David Letterman. "Round Here."

- December 11, 1996 - The Late Show With David Letterman. "Catapult."

- December 12, 1996 - The Late Show With David Letterman. "A Long December."

- April 10, 1997 - The Tonight Show With Jay Leno. "Daylight Fading."

- June 21, 1997 - VH1 Broadcast from Rockfest. "Daylight Fading" and "Catapult."

- August 12, 1997 - VH1 Storytellers. "A Long December," "Angels of the Silences," "Mr. Jones," "Rain King," "Catapult," "Have You Seen Me Lately?," and "Ghost Train."

- November 6, 1997 - MTV Live From the 10 Spot. "Recovering the Satellites," "Angels of the Silences," "Rain King," "Goodnight Elisabeth," "Catapult," "Mr. Jones," "Omaha," "Sullivan Street," "Have You Seen Me

Lately?," "Round Here," "I'm Not Sleeping," "A Murder of One," "Anna Begins," "A Long December," and "Walkaways."

- July 24, 1999 - Pay-Per-View Broadcast from Woodstock. "Mr. Jones," "Angels of the Silences," "Rain King," "Anna Begins," "Omaha," "Recovering the Satellites," "Round Here," "Hanginaround," "A Long December," "Have You Seen Me Lately?," and "A Murder of One."

- October 9, 1999 - VH1 Broadcast from Netaid. "St. Robinson In His Cadillac Dream," "Rain King," and "Hanginaround."

- November 4, 1999 - Late Night With Conan O'Brien. "Hanginaround."

- November 18, 1999 - The Late Show With David Letterman. "Hanginaround."

- February 9, 2000 - The Tonight Show With Jay Leno. "Kid Things."

- August 25, 2000 - CNN's ShowBiz Today. "All My Friends."

- Matt, Charlie, and Ben appeared twice on The Tonight Show with Jewel as her back-up band.

7
Live
Quotes

- Before "Round Here," November 19, 1999 in Columbus, Ohio: "There comes this time when you gotta figure out, am I really going to be a musician or am I really going to be a dishwasher? Some people decide, well, I'm a musician no matter what or I'm a painter no matter what or I'm an actor. They do it anyway forever because it doesn't really matter if you're huge or not but you've got to make that decision. Everyone else in your life is telling you to get on with it or go back to school or get a better job. There's nothing wrong with that but you've got to make that decision because every day is doubt and every day is confusion for everybody, including all of us."

- Before playing "Omaha" on November 24, 1999 in Chicago, Illinois: "I used to have a Japanese fighting fish. Have you ever had fish? Anyone ever had fish? I had this Japanese fighting fish and I loved it so much. It was the coolest fish. Then I got a goldfish and my sister put it in the bowl with the Japanese fighting fish. The goldfish ate the Japanese fighting fish and killed it. I was so upset that I wrote this song and I named it after that fish. You've probably heard it before."

- Before "Mercury" on July 17, 1999 in Kalamazoo, Michigan: "This is a song about a truly messed up chic; the kind of chic that is so messed up that she messes you up. It's either that or you were already so messed up to be even dealing with a chic like this. That's probably more likely the case. You know, like, when you're so just completely addicted to woman who is so... bad. It's like things got inside her and bent and twisted and things inside her wrapped and twisted around the bent and twisted things. When you get near her, she reaches out and grabs you and bends and twists and it's so... fucked... up. But you're just so stuck with it and you need it really, really bad. She says one thing and does another and she changes all the time because she's just like mercury."

- "This is a little chestnut that features the guitar and vocal styling of one Mr. Dan Vickrey." -Adam on July 6, 1999 before "Daylight Fading."

- "We're actually really proud that we got this song together because it's a bitch to play." - Adam on October, 13 1999 in London before the first live performance of "I Wish I Was A Girl."

- Before debuting "Closer to You" at the May 5, 2000 Shim Sham show in New Orleans, LA: "Me and some friends, we wrote all of these songs for this movie called 'Josie and the Pussycats' a few weeks ago. It was our favorite cartoon when we were kids so we wrote a bunch of songs for it. We wrote seven songs in seven days. We wrote the first song on a Friday night when we were having a party at my house. The next Friday, we were getting ready to have another party. We had written seven songs and I got in the shower and thought, 'Man, I wish I had written a song for Andre to play on' because we all live together. So I went and took a shower and thought of this trumpet line in the shower so I ran out of the shower in a robe to Andre's room and said, 'Get the fuck out of your room, man, I got a song for you!' So he came running across and we spent the first half of the party running up in my bedroom and working on this song."

Section
Four

MISCELLANEOUS

One has to wonder wonder what it feels like to be a member of Counting Crows and to see thousands of faces inspired by your music singing every word and moving with every note. The energy the audience bounces back must be a million times greater than the energy you put out.

Online Resources

1 - Web Sites

- http://www.countingcrows.com - The official Counting Crows site. It is a Flash-enhanced site with a Discography, Band Info, Tour Dates and ticket information, News and Events section, message board, and downloadable photos, desktops, postcards, and "Flashbooks."

- http://www.annabegins.com - Lisa's Counting Crows Shrine. The most comprehensive Crows site on the Internet. It includes a news section, sound files, video files, a huge photograph collection, e-mail postcards, articles, tour reviews, chat room, song interpretations, and much more.

- http://www.countingcrowsdirect.com - Official Counting Crows merchandise site. Music, apparel, collectibles, accessories, and auctions. They also post live mp3s for download.

- http://www.countingcrows-l.org - The home of Counting Crows-L, an unofficial Counting Crows e-mail list. Includes list commands (including how to subscribe), member profiles, a comprehensive tour archive, and a post archive.

- http://come.to/ccfaq - Frequently Asked Questions site. A great FAQ that is updated frequently, Crow site links, articles, and an archive of Adam's posts to America Online.

- http://www.enteract.com/~rfuss/ccboots.html - Counting Crows Bootleg Guide. Lists set lists and venue information of nearly every Counting Crows bootleg that exists. Also includes a FAQ and bootleg reviews.

- http://come.to/ccbooth - The Counting Crows Listening Booth. A very well put-together website with sound files, lyrics, photos, links, and more.

- http://www.geocities.com/digitalcountingcrows - Digital Counting Crows. The definitive resource for live digital recordings of Counting Crows. Maintains an e-mail discussion group for fair distribution of high-quality recordings.

- http://www.gimmyimmy.com - David Immergluck fan site. The one and only site dedicated to the talented band member. Includes his musical history, photographs, and current David news.

- http://www.himalayans.com - Himalayans, A Musical Shrine. Comprehensive site about one of Adam's former bands, Himalayans. Contains lyrics, bios, mp3s, and information on ordering Himalayans' demo tape with Adam on lead vocals.

- http://www.thehimalayans.com - Himalayans Home Page. Created by former band member Dan Jewett. Includes lyrics, photos, and information on ordering the band's demo tape.

- http://www.mediatrip.com/music/radio/64.html - Devil & the Bunny Show. Monthly online radio show hosted by

Adam Duritz and David Immergluck. The two play their favorite music, have special guests, and discuss their musical selections.

- http://www.robards.org/marc/crows/index.html - Counting Crows Theme Page. Download a free Counting Crows theme for your computer.

- http://www.acrossawire.com - The Contrast of White on White. Contains a photo album, lyrics, a message board, and a great archive of both sound and video clips from various performances.

- http://www.bestweb.net/~shame/main.htm - Counting Crows CD-aRtchive. Archive of cover art for various live Counting Crows shows.

11 - Tour Mate Links

Links to sites dedicated to bands that have toured with Counting Crows in the past:

- **Joe 90:** http://www.joe90.net and http://www.neuroticbuffet.com/joe90/
- **Peter Stuart:** http://www.peterstuart.com
- **Dog's Eye View:** http://www.sonymusic.com/artists/DogsEyeView/
- **Cracker:** http://www.crackersoul.com
- **Galactic:** http://www.galacticfunk.com
- **Live:** http://www.friendsoflive.com
- **The Wallflowers:** http://www.thewallflowers.com
- **Arid:** http://www.aridcentral.com
- **Cake:** http://www.cakemusic.com

III - Online Discussions

- Usenet newsgroup: alt.music.counting-crows

- America Online Folder - Keyword: MMC; Look under "Alternative Bands A - F."

- CountingCrows.com Message Board - http://countingcrowsbbs.artistdirect.com/

- MediaTrip Counting Crows Message Board - Go to http://www.mediatrip.com/community/index.html and look for the Counting Crows link.

- Counting Crows-L E-Mail Discussion Group: Send an email to listserv@listserv.aol.com with SUBSCRIBE COUNTINGCROWS-L in the body of the message to subscribe.

2
Random
Facts

Counting Crows band members come out after nearly every show to sign autographs and talk to fans. They usually hang out around their tour buses.

When Universal and PolyGram merged, many employees at Counting Crows' record company, Geffen, were laid off. A lot of these positions were taken over by Interscope Records, the label of Fred Durst of Limp Bizkit.

"Margery Dreams of Horses" was written by Adam aboard a plane in 1989 while flying back from Europe to see Dave Bryson.

Counting Crows' official website won the Best MTV/Yahoo Band Website in 1996.

The band broke up in their early years.

They record all of their shows.

They have played under the aliases "Matt Loves Blossom," "Trial By Fire," "An MTV Band Whose Singer Is a Leo," "The Shatners," and "The No Brainers."

They were originally slated to be the September 1997 VH1 "Artist of the Month" but were replaced by Elton John.

The name "Counting Crows" comes from an old English divination that compares the flimsiness of everything to counting crows.

Famous fans include David Letterman, Melissa Joan Hart, Rider Strong, Gillian Anderson, Jeremy Dean (keyboardist) of Nine Days, and Hanson.

Nine different labels wanted to sign Counting Crows at the beginning of their career.

"Baby, I'm a Big Star Now" was featured in the movie *Rounders* but did not appear on the soundtrack.

A major issue during the late 2000 amphitheatre tour with Live was addressed by Adam in an online sound clip on the band's official website (www.countingcrows.com). Both Counting Crows and Live were originally slated to play 75 minute sets; however, due to certain changes in start and end times at the venues, this didn't end up happening at many shows. Many fans (of both bands) were upset so Adam addressed the Counting Crows fans and explained the problems that they had encountered.

Counting Crows' 1994 performance of "Round Here" on David Letterman occured during the famous "Madonna and Dave" episode during which Madonna stormed off stage. According to Adam, the band didn't get to meet Madonna that night.

Adam Duritz and David Immergluck have appearances in Sordid Humor's "Barbarossa" video.

Section
Five

PHOTOGRAPHS

Adam Duritz singing during The Wallflowers' "Sixth
Avenue Heartache"
June 17, 1997. Long Island, NY. Jones Beach
(c) Frank Deriso

Adam Duritz singing "Serious Drugs" with Gigolo
Aunts
March 5, 1999. New York, NY. Bowery Ballroom
(c) Frank Deriso

Adam Duritz and Dan Vickrey
July 20, 1999. Providence, RI. Lupo's Heartbreak Hotel
(c) Frank Deriso

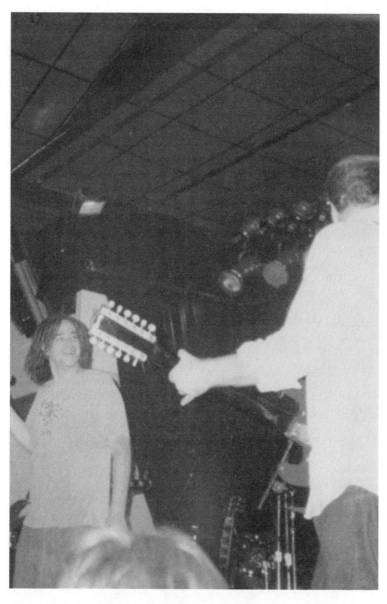

Counting Crows & Gigolo Aunts singing "So You
Wanna Be a Rock n' Roll Star"
July 19, 1999. Sea Bright, NJ. Tradewinds
(c) Frank Deriso

Adam Duritz introducing Gigolo Aunts
July 24, 1999. Rome, NY. Woodstock
(c) Susan Pelletier

Matt Malley & Adam Duritz
October 28, 1999. Washington, DC. 9:30 Club
(c) Martin Lueders

Dan Vickrey & Adam Duritz
October 28, 1999. Washington, DC. 9:30 Club
(c) Martin Lueders

Adam Duritz
October 28, 1999. Washington, DC. 9:30 Club
(c) Martin Lueders

Adam Duritz
October 28, 1999. Washington, DC. 9:30 Club
(c) Martin Lueders

Adam Duritz
October 28, 1999. Washington, DC. 9:30 Club
(c) Martin Lueders

Adam Duritz
October 28, 1999. Washington, DC. 9:30 Club
(c) Martin Lueders

Adam Duritz
October 28, 1999. Washington, DC. 9:30 Club
(c) Martin Lueders

Adam Duritz
October 28, 1999. Washington, DC. 9:30 Club
(c) Martin Lueders

Adam Duritz
October 28, 1999. Washington, DC. 9:30 Club
(c) Martin Lueders

Adam Duritz
October 28, 1999. Washington, DC. 9:30 Club
(c) Martin Lueders

Dan Vickrey & Matt Malley
November 16, 1999. Detroit, MI. State Theater
(c) Don Helinski

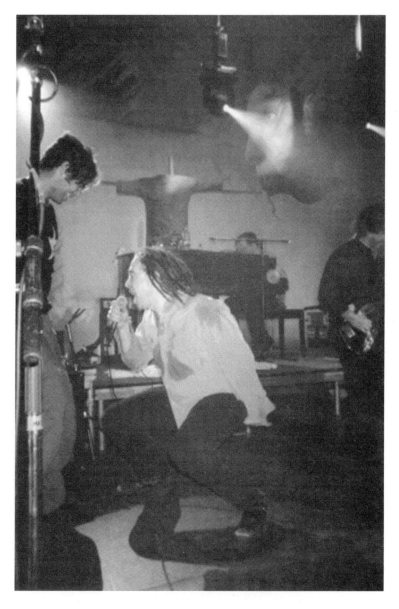

Adam Duritz and Chris Seefried of Joe 90
November 16, 1999. Detroit, MI. State Theater
(c) Don Helinski

Afterword

It's been a long and stressful road writing this book and I know that this is only the beginning. I have tried my best to make this book as error-free as possible but I know there are bound to be mistakes. If you happen to catch any, please send me an email so that they can be corrected in the next version. Or if you'd simply like to talk Counting Crows, I'm here for that too.

Near the end of the book, you'll find two pages about an organization called Scottish International Relief. This is a wonderful charity that's very close to the heart of Martin Lueders, the photographer of the cover photograph and eleven of the interior photographs. Please take the time to read about this wonderful organization and see if you can help out.

Thanks for reading.

Jessica Roop
crowtalk@yahoo.com

The
References

Aldridge, David. "Ben Mize." *Drum!* February – March 1997: 52 – 60.

AMG All Music Guide. 25 Oct 1999 <http://www.allmusic.com>

Broadcast Music, Inc. 12 Dec 1999 <http://www.bmi.com>

Chandler, Jere. "Ben Mize from Counting Crows." *Rewind*. 7 Oct 1999 <http://members.aol.com/jerec7/crows.html>

Copley, Rich. "Former university student comes home with Count ing Crows." *Athenaeum*. 5 Dec 1999 <http://www.athens newspapers.com/weekend/207.crows.html>

Counting Crows-L. 23 Feb 2000 <http://www.countingcrows-l. org>

Counting Crows live chat transcript. MTV Online: 1996. 5 Sept 1999 <http://www.countingcrows.com/aolchat.html>

Counting Crows Set to Release First Studio Album in Three Years; National Tour Kicks Off October 26 in Atlanta. 4 Oct 1999 <http://www.musicnewswire.com/pr/ 99090415153927926>

Crampton, Luke and Rees, Dafydd. *Encyclopedia of Rock Stars*. New York City: Dorling   Kindersley Limited, 1996.

Dana, Sam. "Adam Duritz – Singer-Songwriter/Movie Producer." *Wall of Sound*. 1 Sept 1999 <http://wallofsound.go.com/ news/stories/2616index.html>

Ellis, Andy. "Smashing the Sound Barrier: Counting Crows' David Bryson and Dan Vickrey Break with Convention." *Guitar Player* March 2000: 71 – 80.

Elwood, Philip. "Chris Isaak, Primus top Bammie ballot; 17th show honors Bay Area Musicians on March 5." *The San Francisco Examine*. December 2, 1993: D-1.

Fuss, Richard. *Counting Crows Bootleg Guide*. 23 Feb 2000 <http://www.enteract.com/rfuss/ccboots.html>

Gulla, Bob. "Counting Crows – Bryson and Vickrey play straight to the heart of American pop." *Guitar Magazine Online*. 1 Sept 1999 <http://www.guitarmag.com/issues/9702/9702.ccrows.html>

Hay, Carla. "Counting Crows Explore New Territory." *Billboard Online*. 1 Nov 1999 <http://www.billboard.com/feature/crows.html>

"How does your garden grow?" August 18, 1997 *FFWD Weekly*. 7 Oct 1999 <http://www.greatwest.ca/ffwd/Issues/1997/0828/mus2.html>

iMAGAZINE Interview. 2 Oct 1999 <http://www.thei.aust.com/isite/ctcrows.html>

Information Please – Counting Crows. 7 Oct 1999 <http://cbs.infoplease.com/ipea/A0763394.html>

Isola, Gregory. "Counting Crows' Matt Malley: Charity Before Chops." *Bass Player* October 1994: 9.

LegitCrit. "Exclusive Interview With Adam Duritz of Counting Crows." *KNC Software Entertainment*. 25 Oct 1999 <http://www.kncsoftware.com/knc3new/html/Entertainment/CrowsInterview.htm>

Martin, Steve J. Home page. 23 Oct 1999 <http://www.sjmsoft.com/resume.html>

Modern Rock Live. Interview. With Tom Calmaro. AMFM Radio Network. New York. 19 Jan 1997.

Modern Rock Live. Interview. With Max Tolcoff. AMFM Radio Network. New York. 12 July 1998.

Nichols, Natalie. "As the Crows Flew." *Los Angeles Times* October 13, 1996.

Rage Rules As Mariah, Lil' Wayne, WWF, Counting Crows, And Foos Hit Chart. 10 Nov 1999 <http://mtv.com/news/headlines/991110/story8.html>

Rockline. Interview. With Riki Rachtman. AMFM Radio Network. Los Angeles. 20 Jan 1997.

Smith, Dakota. *Woodstock Feature*. 23 July 1999 <http://www.mediabay.com/woodstock/feat_am.asp?ID=6>

Swartz, Gary. "Not All Crows Fly the Shortest Distance." *Drop-D Magazine* 28 Mar 1997 <Reprinted on http://www.countingcrows.com>

The Usual – Supporting Band for Counting Crows Tour. 5 Sept 1999 <http://www.jol.co.za>

Uhelszki, Jaan. "Counting Crows Counting the Days Until Their Next Album." *Addicted to Noise*. 22 July 1999 <http://www.addict.com/ATN/Music_News_Of_The_World/95-07-08.html#CROWS>

Uhelszki, Jaan. "How Success Spoiled Adam Duritz." *San Fran cisco Chronicle Datebook* October 27 – November 2, 1996: 40 – 41.

Uhelszki, Jaan. "Putting On Duritz." *MSN Music Central*. 1 Sept 1999 <http://musiccentral.msn.com>

Vaziri, Aidin. "Q&A With Adam Duritz." *San Francisco Chronicle Online*. 1 Sept 1999 <http://www.sfgate.com/cgi-bin/article.cgi?file=/chronicle/archive/1998/07/12/PK76769.DTL>

Wild, David. "Bird on a Wire." *Rolling Stone* June 30, 1994: 46 – 82.

All Billboard chart information is from Joel Whitburn's Record Research publications, which chronicle the complete history of American popular music and entertainment based on the Billboard charts. For complete information visit their Web site at http://www.recordresearch.com.

My
Acknowledgments

Writing this book has been full of struggles and triumphs and I know many more are to come. I could not have gotten this far without the support and inspiration of so many amazing people:

My parents for seeing my dream and letting me run with it. This experience has been one I'll never forget. I also thank you for putting up with my love of concerts and my need to travel to see all of these amazing bands.

Kathy White, Honora Thorson, Kristin Thomas, and Lisa Lebarre for being my ever-so-helpful proofreaders. Lisa, you're truly the queen of AnnaBegins.com. It's been great knowing you since your site was "just another" Counting Crows site.

All of my special friends on the "Official Unofficial Counting Crows newsgroup." You guys have been there since the beginning and I adore all of you for it.

Marty Lueders for your stunning photograph on the front cover and several of the interiors photos. I appreciate all of your guidance and wisdom.

Gary, Craig, Chris, and Adam from Joe 90 for all of your stunning concerts, pep talks, and friendships. You have made a great impact in my life and I cannot thank you enough for that. The best of luck to all of you.

To all of my beautiful friends out there in the world, thank you for believing in me. I owe it all to you. You are the ones who have believed in me, regardless of whether or not

I was running in the right direction. Thank you for spending the time to get to know me.

Brittany, thank you for all of the hard work you put into the first version of the first few chapters. I'm so sorry it didn't work out the way we wanted it to, but at least you know it *is* finally out there for fans to enjoy. You are an angel.

Finally, thank you to Counting Crows, especially Adam, for being so supportive and helpful in the creation of this book. Your generosity has been such an inspiration.

About the Cover Photographer
Martin Lueders

Martin Lueders is an internationally recognized, award-winning freelance photographer who specializes in features, editorial and documentary work, primarily on environmental and humanitarian issues. His photographs have been exhibited and published extensively in the U.S. and Europe. Lueders' clients include Greenpeace (International and U.S.A.), Scottish International Relief, Catholic News Service, Catholic Relief Services and Earth Day. His work has been published in *TIME*, *Playboy* (Tokyo), *The Independent on Sunday* (U.K.), *Automobile Magazine*, The Chicago Tribune and The Suddeutsche Zeitung (Munich).

In 1999, Lueders was commissioned by The U.S. Agency For International Development and The Displaced Children & Orphans Fund to document child soldiers in four African countries for a traveling exhibit and book entitled, "Playing For Keeps: Children & War in Africa," which includes 36 black-and-white photographs and testimonies from current and former child combatants.

In 1999, he moved to the Washington, D.C.-area with his wife and three children after having resided on the west coast of Scotland since 1992.

Lueders is currently working on contracts with the U.S. Census Bureau and the documentary project, Chicago In the Year 2000.

For more information, Martin Lueders can be reached at:
email: insightphotos@hotmail.com
tel: (301) 926-4818

A Few Important Words About Scottish International Relief

"A peasant must stand a long time on a hillside with his mouth open before a roast duck flies in."
– Chinese Proverb

SIR began in 1992 when their initial effort to deliver one small load of aid to Bosnia gave birth to an organization which today, everyday, brings hope to thousands of desperately poor people in Eastern Europe, Africa and South America. Sometimes this hope arrives in the form of a truck bulging with vital donated aid; sometimes in the form of health care provided by one of their medical projects. Often it just takes the form of a bowl of soup given to an abandoned child.

SIR's work depends on ordinary folk whose generosity and hard graft produces incredible results. Virtually all of the aid SIR sends overseas is donated by the public and nearly all the work they do to collect, categorize and transport the aid is carried out by volunteers. Volunteers are also responsible for most of their fund-raising – much of which is carried out through their charity shops. School children, long-term unemployed people, those with disabilities, the elderly – in fact, people from all walks of life – play an active role in what they do. Some work in their warehouses or drive their vans; others help in their shops and offices or help organize fundraising events. There are also thousands of people who support SIR's work by donating goods or money.

LIBERIA, in West Africa, has recently endured a seven year civil war that devastated an already poverty stricken country. Here, in addition to sending regular shipments of high value aid, they are also helping the people in other ways. SIR funds a mobile health clinic that provides primary health care for 60,000 people who previously had none. They are also working on projects that will improve living conditions for people living in a leper colony and those who are blind. They also supply computers and tools for a training projects.

CROATIA may now be free from war, but tens of thousands of people – many of them refugees who have no prospect of returning to their homes – continue to live in terrible conditions. Most of the aid SIR sends here is distributed by a group called the Family Centre. They work with both refugee and local families who endure abject poverty. They also help returning refugees whose old homes have been looted and damaged during the war. SIR provides tools and household goods to enable these people to begin their lives again. The Family Centre gives SIR's aid to people in need regardless of which ethnic group they belong to.

ROMANIA continues to endure horrendous social and economic problems. Overcrowded, understaffed hospitals and orphanages are home to tens of thousands of abandoned, sick children. Here SIR sends lorry loads of desperately needed medical aid, toiletries and clothes to a town called Tirgu Mures. They are also setting up a small children's home that will care for ten children who are HIV positive and who have been abandoned by their parents. In addition to this they run a soup kitchen that provides some gypsy children with the only hot meals they ever receive.

BOLIVIA, in South America, is also home to thousands of street kids who have been abandoned by their parents. Here SIR helps to fund a small home that cares for 25 of these children.

S.I.R. is currently accepting donations and fundraising ideas in order to found a Washington, D.C.-based division to further implement their work. If you would like to make a donation to this charity, please contact them at:

Web: http://www.excellence.co.uk/~sir/sir.html
Mailing Address: SIR; 1 Devon Place; St. Andrews Industrial Estate; Pollockshaws Road; GLASGOW; G41 1RD; Scotland

ORDER FORM

Books
___ Copies of *Crow Talk: The Definitive Guide to Counting Crows* at $14.95

Posters
___ 18x24 Posters of the Crow Talk cover photo (live at the 9:30 Club in Washington, DC) at $7.99

Shipping
Books: $3.50 for the first book; $1.50 for each additional
Posters: $4.00 for the first poster; $2.00 for each additional
International Shipping: Add $2.00 to each shipping price. Please send payment in U.S. funds only.

Payment Options:
Check or Money Order: Please send the total amount to the address below.

Rocket Ride Press
PO Box 842
Hilliard, Ohio 43026
USA

Please add sales tax if you are located in Ohio.

Credit Card: You may pay via credit card (Visa, MasterCard, Discover, or American Express) on our web site only at www.rocketridepress.com.

ORDER FORM

Books
___ Copies of *Crow Talk: The Definitive Guide to Counting Crows* at $14.95

Posters
___ 18x24 Posters of the Crow Talk cover photo (live at the 9:30 Club in Washington, DC) at $7.99

Shipping
Books: $3.50 for the first book; $1.50 for each additional
Posters: $4.00 for the first poster; $2.00 for each additional
International Shipping: Add $2.00 to each shipping price. Please send payment in U.S. funds only.

Payment Options:
Check or Money Order: Please send the total amount to the address below.

Rocket Ride Press
PO Box 842
Hilliard, Ohio 43026
USA

Please add sales tax if you are located in Ohio.

Credit Card: You may pay via credit card (Visa, MasterCard, Discover, or American Express) on our web site only at www.rocketridepress.com.